# CATS

## a Feline Compendium

Fenella Smith
and
The Brothers McLeod

⬛ SQUARE PEG

1 3 5 7 9 10 8 6 4 2

Square Peg, an imprint of Vintage,
20 Vauxhall Bridge Road,
London SW1V 2SA

Square Peg is part of the Penguin Random House
group of companies whose addresses can be found at
global.penguinrandomhouse.com.

Penguin
Random House
UK

First published by Square Peg in 2017

Penguin.co.uk/vintage


A CIP catalogue record for this book is available from
the British Library

ISBN 9781910931363

Printed and bound in China by C&C Offset Printing
Co. Ltd.

Penguin Random House is committed to a sustainable
future for our business, our readers and our planet.
This book is made from Forest Stewardship Council®
Certified paper.

MIX
Paper from
responsible sources
FSC® C018179
FSC
www.fsc.org

'A black cat crossing your path signifies that the animal is going somewhere.'

Groucho Marx

We three siblings had many pets in our childhood home, but the first was a cat. And the second, third and fourth. The first was a beautiful tortoiseshell called Perky, named after a children's television character (which was a pig; don't ask me to explain it!). Perky predated me and so it seemed as if she had always been there. I don't have strong memories of her anymore, but I do recall a sense of confusion when one day she never came home. Like a lot of felines, her kidneys failed and she didn't make it to her twelfth birthday.

Eager not to let the house go pet-free, our parents bought another cat. He was a big tabby cat whom we called Tigger (another children's character; this time more cat-related). I loved Tigger so much. He was my buddy, my animal companion for a long time. He was also a complete and utter homicidal maniac. No amount of discouragement from us could quell his natural instincts. He wasn't afraid of anything – he once scared off a fox. He may have scared off a herd of bison for all I know; I wouldn't be surprised. But he was also very loving. I loved to heap affection on him and he loved to receive it. I think he considered me worthy of keeping alive and that means a lot to me. Tigger's long gone now, but I remember him every time I meet a new cat and stop to give them a bit of fuss.

My sister Fenella and I have really enjoyed researching and writing this book, uncovering more about the breeds of cat we know, and discovering others we had never heard about. It's clear that cats have made a great impact on human life and culture all around the world. In fact, we've included a few mythological felines amongst the real ones (as well as a few other surprises).

We've also had fun creating a dictionary of cat terms. These are things that all cat owners will recognise, but for which there has been no single dictionary word (until now).

As in our book about dog breeds, we have had the pleasure of working with an extremely talented illustrator. He's worked with Disney, Aardman, and the BBC among others. The fact he's also our older brother Greg is another bonus!

This book is dedicated to cats, and to all those that love them and live with them.

Myles McLeod

Our childhood cat, Tigger, terrified me slightly. He had a certain wildness to him that made me rather in awe of him. I remember one occasion when I was sitting on my parents' bed while Tigger slept peacefully underneath it. I decided I wanted to play so I woke him up, removed one of my socks, and then dangled it from my perch, watching his blade-like claws swiping for it. I managed to wind him up so much that before long I realised I was stranded on this island of a bed, lest he grab my leg as I retreated. Our mother had to rescue me!

Tigger has legend status in our family. I was so sad when he didn't come home one day; he was all old and knotty like an over-loved teddy in the end. My musings here always have him and his wondrous soul in mind.

Fenella Smith.

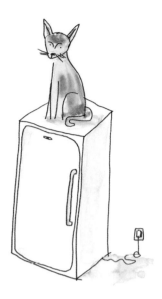

## Abyssinian

Resembles the African wildcat, the ancestor of domesticated felines. Very loyal, but don't expect them to sit on your lap for too long: they have too much energy. If you lose an Abyssinian, just check all the high places like the top of the fridge. You'll soon find that they've been watching you look for them all along.

## Aegean

These Greek islanders have been sorting out their own breeding programme for decades, which may explain their lack of genetic problems and general good health. Naturally, they are lovers of fish and fishing.

## American Bobtail

These loyal, short-tailed cats are big on brains and love to play. It is for this reason that they are banned from casinos (probably). They can be trained to walk on a leash, but watch out: those brains of theirs also make them experts at escapology.

## American Curl

If you ever wondered what an affectionate, kid-friendly cat might look like if it faced into a strong breeze, then check out the Curl. Their ears literally curl backwards! The long-haired variety have a plumed tail too, as if curly ears weren't enough to show off about.

## American Shorthair

The quintessential all-rounder.
Descended from 'working cats'
brought over the Atlantic on ships
with the first American settlers. Do
they still like boats? We like to think
these days they prefer a yachting
vacation off the Hamptons.

## American Wirehair

Sounds like a cowboy nickname, right? The Wirehair used to be the Shorthair, but that wasn't tough enough for it. Thanks to a genetic mutation, the first Wirehair appeared in Verona, New York in 1966 and has been going strong ever since.

zzZZZZZZZ

## Arabian Mau

This natural breed has been
sleeping its way through 1000 years
of hot desert days in the Arabian
Peninsula. It prefers to be active in
the cooler nights. How sensible!

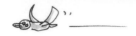

<u>Arabian sand cat</u>
(wild cat)
Very rarely seen (in fact no one
saw one between 2006 and 2016!),
this feline is perfectly adapted to the
desert. It doesn't even need to drink.
It finds all the water it needs in the
birds, mammals and reptiles that it
eats. Ugh! It is very cute though so,
you know, swings and roundabouts.

## Australian Mist

One of the few animals from Australia that isn't deadly (and one of a handful of cat breeds that originate there). Friendly, intelligent cats who will happily overeat if you let them. Time to get a lock for your fridge? And your BBQ!

## Balinese

Long glossy hair. Slender elegant figures... these pussycats are the supermodels of the meowing world. Smart and affectionate, they also have a tendency towards acrobatics. They annoy quite a lot of other cats on account of their perfection.

## Bastet
(religious cat)

Bastet was one of the gods of Ancient Egypt. She was initially revered as a war goddess with the head of a lioness. A few thousand years later, she had the head of a small cat and was considered the goddess of perfume. It's tough at the top.

## Bengal

If you're after a pet leopard that won't eat you, the Bengal may be the answer. Selective crossbreeding between domestic cats and the wild Asian leopard cat created this distinctive and beautiful cat. They have a fondness for water and can jump high, so be vigilant of felines preparing to swan-dive when you run that relaxing bath.

## Birman
A beautiful cat with white gloves and striking eyes. Birmans are sociable, interactive cats and will join in wherever possible - including reading your paper, or typing on your computer. Legend has it that these Burmese temple cats carried the souls of their priests on the final journey to paradise. Could be useful?

## Bombay

Hypnotically beautiful eyes. Shiny
black fur. This little homage to a
panther will charm you with their
sociable and playful ways. Some
can be trained to do tricks and walk
on a lead. Happy to live with other
cats as long as they have agreed
their pecking order within the
household.

## Brazilian Shorthair

No, this is not a special haircut for ladies (ahem!). These large, snuggly cats are descended from Portuguese felines brought over to Brazil in the 1500s.

## British Shorthair

An old-fashioned sort of Brit. Reserved, mild-tempered, quiet and faithful. Probably the sort of cat that would host a very exclusive and polite cocktail party. Most often comes in a delightful blue hue.

## Burmese

These incredibly cute cats have wonderfully large eyes, and equally large hearts. They love to be involved with family life. Burmese are eager to try out door handles, light pulls and bin lids and will happily sit on your keyboard while you work and try to 'help'.

## Burmilla

Legend has it that the Burmilla exists due to a tryst between a Chinchilla Persian and Lilac Burmese in the 1980s. This breed has a regal air and a beautiful silver coat, which they may or may not allow you to groom depending on their mood.

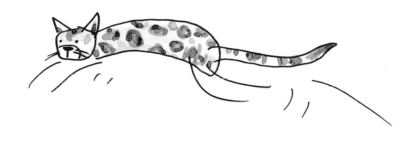

## California Spangled

Bred to resemble wild cats like the leopard, these dappled frisky felines love to chase and jump - so keep your valuables glued down!

<u>Caracal</u>
(wild cat)
These medium-sized moggies roam
(and jump impressively) across
harsh African habitats, looking for
tasty morsels by night. Their black
ear-tufts resemble misplaced,
comedy eyebrows.

## Chartreux

This smiling blue cat isn't actually French at all, but Persian in origin. Legend has it they came west with the returning crusaders and became a regular feature in French monasteries, including the Grande Chartreuse monastery, where they picked up their name.

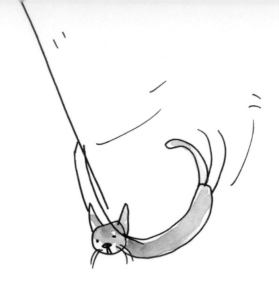

<u>Chausie</u>

Pronounced chow-see, this athletic beast is descended from both domestic felines and the wild Jungle cat of Egypt and South Asia. It's basically the Tarzan of the cat world.

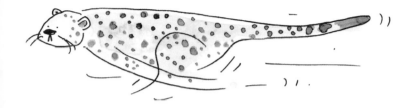

## Cheetah

(big cat)

This spotted speeder can reach speeds of up to 70mph. They are a threatened species - let's hope they can outrun extinction! They are not quite solitary and not quite sociable, but rather a bit of both. I think we can all relate to that.

## Cheetoh

No-one's sure what happened to the
Cheeteh, the Cheetih and the
Cheetuh, but this fierce-looking
beast is actually a real...well...
er...pussycat.

## Chinchilla

A cat named after a rodent doesn't seem like a good prospect, but this Persian breed with thick white hair and green eyes (and, apparently, black eye liner) is a beauty. You need to enjoy grooming if you want one of these though, or you may eventually lose them in a giant ball of fur.

## Clippercat

These New Zealanders have a few more toes than your average cat. Apparently in the old days people would give ships' captains 'polydactyl' cats, so perhaps that's how they travelled so far. Thinking about it, a few extra claws could be handy for holding on during a sea storm! Cats with too many toes have been reported from around the globe, and folklore suggests that they make the best mousers, and the best familiars for witches!

Clouded leopard
(big cat)
This beautiful small 'big cat' (or is
that big 'small cat'?) has an
exceptionally long tail: great for
keeping its balance! Perhaps this is
a clue to why they are so rarely
seen?

## Colourpoint Shorthair
The Siamese-related Colourpoint is a chatty cat. They don't stop talking. Not ever. That's right. They're still talking. Right now. And now. And now. And probably even when they're asleep.

## Cornish Rex

For once the name is accurate. These curly-haired, whippet-shaped cats originate in Cornwall. The original Cornish Rex was born in 1950 and named Kallibunker. Keen to produce more kittens like him, his human counterparts ensured he was bred back with his mother. The things that go on in the country!

## Cougar
(big cat)

Yes, it's not just a term for predatory women of mature years. Though it's a big cat (also known as the puma or mountain lion), the cougar is actually more related to our smaller feline companions. Just wondering though, would an older cougar female that likes younger cougar males be termed a 'cougar cougar'?

## Cymric

Ever wondered what the offspring of
a cat and a fluffy rabbit would look
like? The answer is the tailless,
placid Cymric (pronounced *kim-rick*,
don't you know!).

## Devon Rex

Now, this breed might not win the beauty contest, but they are playful and smart. Their behaviour is often compared to monkeys and dogs. They love, love, love food and are experts at the 'I've not eaten for weeks' face.

## Donskoy

This wrinkly Russian cat comes in
four states of undress, from slightly
furry to completely bald. They are
super affectionate, but don't like to
be left alone, so if you're going to get
one...well, get two!

## Dragon Li

Known as the Fox Flower Cat in its
native China. Legend, but no
evidence, suggests this breed is
descended from the wild Chinese
mountain cat. Perhaps it should be
renamed the Chinese Dragon
Mountain Fox Flower Legend Cat
just to be on the safe side?

## Egyptian Mau

The stunning Mau has been going strong in Egypt since the time of the Pharaohs. The distinctive spotted coat can be seen depicted on ancient papyri. Now that's a pedigree!

<u>European Burmese</u>
An incredibly loyal breed who will
choose their favourite human, then
scale the tallest bit of furniture in the
house to proclaim their love.

## Exotic Shorthair

This is a short-haired version of the
Persian, although more playful than
their forebears and needing less
grooming. If we were being unkind
we'd say they look a little bit like they
have their face pressed up against a
window (even when there's no
window).

<u>Foldex</u>

Although it sounds like a
trademarked name for a hi-tech
folding machine, this is in fact a
folded-ear breed that originated in
the 1990s in Québec, Canada. Their
wide eyes and thick, fluffy tail are
complemented by a cheerful and
affectionate personality.

## German Rex

This rare breed has curly, silky hair like its Cornish Rex cousin. The mother of the breed, Lämmchen (German for 'little lamb'), was found in a Berlin hospital garden in the years after World War II.

## Havana Brown

What a name! Havana Brown sounds like a film noir detective! Actually it's a comment on their lustrous brown coat (and possibly the colour of Cuban cigars). And if that isn't impressive enough, check out the name of the first cat to officially mark the breed: Elmtower Bronze Idol. Wow.

## Highlander

Despite its name, this breed is not from the north of Scotland, but was bred in the USA. Having said that, this gentle giant of a cat probably does have the lung capacity to play the bagpipes. Their distinctive ears make it look like their heads are permanently attached to a pair of apostrophes.

## Himalayan

The Himmie is a Persian-Siamese cross with stunning blue eyes and Salvador Dali whiskers. They are not an energetic breed, and could probably write a thesis on how to be laid-back if only they weren't so busy relaxing.

Honeybear
This sweet looking cat is supposed
to be the offspring of a Persian
and... wait for it... a skunk! Yeah.
people will believe anything these
days.

<u>Isle of Man Longhair</u>
This is basically a Cymric cat with a
tail. Flaunt it if you've got it baby!

## Jaguar
(big cat)

The jaguar's reputation in Meso-American culture goes back a long way. It was believed that the jaguar could pass between our world and the spirit world. Certainly it seems as happy in the trees as on the ground, and they hunt both day and night, so who knows?

## Japanese Bobtail

An important part of Japanese history and folklore, and associated with good luck. One legend explains the tiny tail: a sleeping cat's tail set on fire and when running away, it accidentally burned down the town. Afterwards, the enraged emperor ordered all cat's tails to be cut short. Hmm... doesn't sound that lucky.

## Khao Manee
Striking white cats with starburst eyes from Thailand, Khao Manee are said to bring long life and title into your house (not sure who for though!).

## Korat

These cats have a beautiful silvery-blue coat that sometimes seems to have a halo! (It's actually because their hairs have silver tips). Both beautiful and benevolent, they are most certainly angelic.

## LaPerm

A wonderful cat that, unlike most
active breeds, is also happy to sit in
your lap. Their textured fur can be
wavy, curly or even tight ringlets.
Added bonus: they don't shed that
much. Having said all that, LaPerm
does sound rather like the villain
from a hairdressing movie.

## Leopard
(big cat)

These wonderfully majestic cats are solitary for the majority of their lives. They are quite fond of swimming, especially if they can catch lunch at the same time.

## Lion
(big cat)
The males get the fancy hairdo and
are considerably larger than their
female companions. These
communal cats may do a couple of
hours of prancing about but spend a
good twenty-one hours a day
snuggled up together, power
napping.

<u>Lynx</u>
(wild cat)
These cats are reputed to have
second sight, and the ability to see
through solid objects. They like to
keep a crystal ball at home, too.
(Also have very cute tufty ears.)

## Maine Coon

These gentle giants are regal in appearance with goofy, loving characters. They will amuse you all day with their playful ways, fluffy paws and huge feather-duster tail. They are the largest domestic cat breed, and are also very good at turning on taps when they fancy a drink. Not so good at turning them off, though.

Manx

The tailless cat from the Isle of Man,
they have hound-like personalities.
Playful and fond of a chat.

## Margay
(wild cat)

We all know that cats love trees, but the wild margay takes this to new heights — literally. Spends virtually all of its life in the tall trees of Central and South America.

Minskin

The Dachshund of the cat world.
Deliberately bred to have short legs
and not much hair. Humans are
weird.

## Moggy

OK, so not an actual 'breed', but the Moggy is perhaps the most common and most loved of all cat varieties. It's any cat of unknown and dubious heritage, probably with a family tree filled with rascals and mousers and notorious criminals like T.S. Eliot's Macavity!

Mouse
HELP! GET ME OUT OF THIS BOOK!

## Munchkin

A controversial breed like the Minskin, they look a little like your favourite cashmere sweater that shrank in the wash. These dinky-legged felines can apparently leap as well as the next puddy cat, though.

## Nebelung

Nebelung translates from German as 'creature of the mist', and is believed to refer to their shimmering blue-grey coats. They are partial to a dramatic entrance with a smoke machine.

## Norwegian Forest Cat

Made for a chilly day, these intelligent and large cats have very thick double coats and are well adapted to living in cold climates. They also have tufted ear-tops (fancy) and long claws. Legend has it that they were originally mountain-dwelling fairy cats, and will happily climb up rock faces.

<u>Ocicat</u>
Looks like a wild cat but won't try to
eat you (unless you wind it up too
much with a piece of string).

<u>Ojos Azules</u>
Spanish for 'blue eyes'. This trait first
appeared in feral cats from New
Mexico. They are almost mythical
thanks to their extreme rarity.

### Oriental

A group of cats including the Shorthair, Longhair and Bicolour that go well with an expensive oriental rug. There's no denying it, these sophisticated looking cats have massive ears — all the better to hear you admiring them with.

Ovinnik
(mythological cat)
If you meet a black cat with burning coals for eyes, don't get on the wrong side of him. It could be Ovinnik, the dangerous spirit of Slav mythology. and he has a penchant for arson.

_Panthera blytheae_
(fossil cat)
The oldest known 'big cat'. This
now-extinct felid lived six million
years ago high up in the cold
Himalayas. It's not known if they
chose Tibet because (a) the local
antelope were tasty or (b) because it
had an excellent reputation for
spiritual enlightenment.

### Pallas's cat
(wild cat)

This wild cat can be identified by its small, rounded ears and general expression of being really rather annoyed. Found mainly in Asia, these cats live in cold, arid places. They are fond of ambushing their prey by waiting outside dens, and have even been sighted partaking in a spot of fishing using their keen claws.

## Persian

The most popular breed. The cat that any visitor to a house immediately wishes to fuss. Outstandingly cute... usually. The cat with the world record for the longest hair was a cross between a Persian and a Himalayan called Colonel Meow. He was less about cute, more about scowl.

## Peterbald

A relatively new breed from Saint Petersburg... or maybe not? If there were cats from outer space then they would probably look like Peterbalds. They are often hairless, with enormous ears, intelligent eyes and a pointed jaw. If this is an alien invasion, then it's a very affectionate one.

## Pittsburgh Refrigerator Cat

This strain of feline has a thick coat
that protects them from
temperatures below minus thirty.
Their whiskers are also longer and
thicker than most cats, allowing
them to navigate in the dark. In
normal temperatures they quickly
die. One final fact: they never
existed, but this urban legend from
nineteenth-century America was
reprinted all over the world as fact!

## Pixie-bob

They have a double coat and a
shortened tail. These unusual cats
are also highly intelligent and can
understand some commands from
their human companions. They have
their own division at MI5.

## Ragamuffin

These are jumbo-sized but genial cats. Great child-friendly pets. If you lose the cat, but discover the doll in your child's stroller is looking especially hairy, you can stop looking.

## Ragdoll

No, this breed is not bald, nor does it
have enormous ears, nor an
especially long tail or extremely
short legs. The Ragdoll is simply a
well proportioned, chilled out, blue-
eyed beauty.

<u>Russian Blue</u>
These divine creatures are,
appropriately enough, also known as
Archangel Cats (thanks to their
possible origin in Arkhangelsk,
northern Russia). Shy with
strangers, but loyal and loving to
their owners - at least when they're
not busy reading Dostoevsky.

## Savannah

A stunning cat. Leggy and long with exotic spots. Their wild looks come from their serval ancestors (a wild cat native to Africa that hunts by night in marshes). These are confident cats! Yes, these beauties know how to work the camera.

## Scottish Fold

Natively Scottish (spotted by a
Scottish shepherd in 1961) with
forward-folded ears. Loyal and
loving but need independence too
(like the Scottish). Their folded ears
give their face a softer, more
rounded appearance...they also fit
through cat flaps more easily.

Scottish wildcat
(wild cat)
Like a tabby cat but with more
muscles.

## Selkirk Rex

If you were being kind you'd say this curly-haired wonder was like a cute, cuddly toy. If you were being cruel you'd say it looked like the first attempts of a trainee taxidermist.

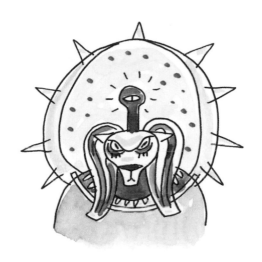

Sekhmet
(religious cat)
A lioness-headed god from Ancient
Egypt responsible for war, violence
and destruction who drew her
powers from the sun. In short, you
wouldn't want to get on the wrong
side of her.

## Siamese

Originating in Thailand, these cats were the treasured pets of royalty. A very communicative, rather strong-minded breed, that adores attention. Pairs may be seen singing and dancing together on the piano.

## Siberian

This strong, friendly feline comes from Russia and has a coat for all seasons. Siberians really do like to fluff up for winter (and shed for spring). They play fetch and can walk on a lead so are sometimes described as 'dog-like', but don't let them hear you say that!

## Singapura

As kittens, they have the look of gremlins. They like heat and high places, but are not so fond of loud noises, so if you arrive with a toddler you may receive a glare and flick of the tail as they exit the room.

## Smilodon
(fossil cat)

These sabre-toothed tigers only
went extinct 10,000 years ago. You
can bet that the cavemen of the day
didn't keep them as pets. These
ferocious-looking cats probably lived
in packs like modern lions. And they
weren't all tooth and claw, because
they also sported a cute bobtail.

## Snow Leopard
(big cat)

Mystery surrounds this rarely-seen big cat. Are they shape-shifting mountain spirits? Or ghosts of the Himalayas? Do they blend in with the icy rocks, or do they become the rocks? Trouble is, they are so good at hiding (even from each other) that when mating season arrives, it can take a while to find a lover!

### Somali

Is it a fox? Is it a little lion? No, it's a Somali. The Somali is best known for its ruddy, semi-long haired coat, though it comes in other colours too. A descendant of the Abyssinian, though neither likes to mention it.

## Sphynx

If you intend to own a Sphynx cat you may also wish to buy it a small selection of clothing. They may be naked but they're not backwards in coming forwards, especially if they are in their favourite piece of knitwear.

<u>Suffolk Chocolate</u>
This new breed is partial to a
saunter round the block with you and
likes to play fetch. Would colour-
match a chocolate Labrador
perfectly if you're after an
aesthetically pleasing household.

## Sumxu

This Chinese breed is extinct. In fact, it may never have existed at all! This mythical beast was said to have lop ears. Think of a cat with floppy lobes like a dog and you're there.

## Suphalak

These copper-coloured cats with golden eyes have been a constant, if rare, inhabitant of Thailand for centuries. They feature in the manuscripts of ancient verse, which is why they are big fans of poetry.

## Tiger
(big cat)
Did you know, each of these ambush predators has its very own stripe pattern. Also, their night vision is six times better than humans'. And they can swim. And lift twice their own bodyweight. Basically don't go near them.

## Tonkinese

The Tonk is a descendant of the
Siamese and Burmese. Their name
comes from the Gulf of Tonkin in the
South China Sea where the cats
once worked as sailors on tiny
galleons (we wish). They love
attention and love to give it back (a
pair is a good idea). But don't dare
to ignore a Tonk or it will find other
ways to entertain itself. Perhaps with
your curtains?

## Toyger

Say 'tiger' in a Birmingham accent and you've got it. Your own personal pet tiger, but in a safe format. This is a relatively new breed, intended to have similar markings to a tiger. Easy to train and rather laid back.

## Turkish Angora

The mischievous Turkish Angora never really stops moving and dancing and pouncing. Some even enjoy swimming, despite their long hair. They are devoted to their human counterparts, but that doesn't mean they won't ambush an exposed big toe for a laugh.

### Turkish Van

Sounds like street food but is in fact
a very rare and ancient breed mainly
found in Russia, Iran, Iraq and
Turkey. A distinctive white coat and
coloured markings, especially on
their tail, really do make them stand
out. Along with their desire to be
high up, they love to play and move
fast, so if you are a collector of
precious ornaments, this adventurer
is not for you.

## Ukrainian Levkoy

This hairless, flop-eared breed may not be the most beautiful, but it's smart and loving. May need sun block when it's hot and a jacket when it's cold. Probably why its ancestors evolved a fur coat. Just saying!

# Cat Dictionary of Terms

There are so many things cats do
that don't have dictionary definitions
that we decided to start a new
cat dictionary!

**Arrogoflash**
The withering look of disgust a cat
gives you to indicate that humans
are not, in their humble opinion, the
most advanced form of life on earth.

<u>Boundfail</u>
A cat leap that is too short for the
intended destination

<u>Cataddict</u>
A cat fancier who keeps more than three cats.

<u>Catanatic</u>
A cat fancier who keeps more than
ten cats.

<u>Catunatic</u>
A cat fancier who has lost count of
how many cats they have.

<u>Catanchored</u>
A cat that is unafraid of anything and remains impassive and immovable even when spotted by a dog (much to the dog's confusion and alarm).

Catloaf

A cat's innate ability to resemble a
loaf of bread by merely tucking away
the front paws.

Catortionism
The feline ability to perfectly fit into
the tiniest place, such as a
saucepan, small box or even, for the
more ambitious, a vase.

<u>Cheatymoggy</u>
'Your' cat that has been regularly
visiting neighbours' houses,
ingratiating itself with nice old ladies.

<u>Cheatyscran</u>
The delicious, expensive food your
Cheattymoggy receives (and
prefers) at your neighbour's house.

**Clawside**
The sideways knowing look your cat
gives you as it sharpens its claws.
'Yes human, they are very, very
pointy.'

<u>Contenticrouch</u>
The snuggly stance and closed-eye
happiness of a cat lapping up a tasty
drink.

## Dangerperch

A cat's favourite place to stand or sit — usually the most ridiculous, perilous or difficult place available. Examples include: on top of your door, on a tiny fence post, on the precipice of a nineteenth-floor balcony.

<u>Dangerquench</u>
The risky business of drinking from
curious and precarious perches
including the edge of the toilet
or bath.

## Deskmeet

The ability of a cat to stop any form
of productive work by sitting on your
computer keyboard and purring
loudly. 'Give ME attention!'

Discohack

The amazing, rippling dance-moves
your cat performs while coughing out
a hairball.

<u>Disgustiprowl</u>
The aloof swagger your cat adopts
to show its disapproval of...well,
almost anything!

<u>Dogbop</u>
The lively crack across an annoying dog's face that has no concept of personal space.

<u>DogbopXL</u>
See Dogbop but with added claws
for an especially persistent or stupid
dog.

<u>Exitworry</u>
The anxiety that your cat expresses
while pacing beside the back door,
desperate to go out.

Exitquibble
The look on your cat's face when it decides not to go out after a bout of Exitworry, but instead decides to just stay where it was, looking at you as though you are an idiot.

Exitquibblefusion
The exasperation you feel when you
re-close the door after the cat has
refused to move after some
Exitquibble, but then notice that your
cat really does want to go out
after all.

<u>Felino-warmer</u>
A recently parked car with a cat sitting
on the still-warm bonnet.

## Flapback

The cautionary awareness of a cat
going through a cat-flap behind
another, intent on avoiding being
whacked in the face by said flap.

<u>Flufflement</u>
The fur you find in your dinner as a
result of the cat'helping'you
prepare supper.

Footflump

The comforting feeling when you are relaxing in bed and can feel a warm, snoozing cat lying across your feet.

<u>Friendfoes</u>
A word that captures the essence of the relationship between any two cats.

Icepadding
The comedy walk your cat does in deep snow.

## Insistimew

The seemingly never-ending meows that your cat makes until you crack open its favourite food.

<u>Kittiglow</u>
The joy of seeing, holding or stroking
a little kitten.

**Kneadiglee**
The comforting feeling of being
rhythmically padded by a cat that
loves you.

<u>Landingluck</u>
Always, and very skilfully, styling out
any clumsy moment by successfully
landing on all four feet and slinking
away casually.

Meowface
The moment before a cat yawns.

<u>Nonchalethal</u>
The breezy yet murderous attitude
exuded by a Catanchored cat
towards any approaching dog.

<u>Overclimber</u>
A cat that is better at climbing things than at working out how to get back down.

<u>Pawpane</u>
Padding at the glass...'let me in.
Pleaaase. Look at my sad face and
cute paws.'

<u>Purrfection</u>
The delight in hearing your beloved cat purr.

<u>Pussession</u>
When a devil possesses your cat
during a visit to the vet.

## Rearflash

The moment you think your cat likes you as it jumps onto your lap for a snuggle but then flashes its bottom perilously close to your face.

## Scentibash

When a cat affectionately rams its head into your face, leg or in fact any other convenient object. This behaviour is actually a way of scent marking and the Internet says it's already got a name: bunting. But we can't find that in our dictionaries and think Scentibash is a much better word!

<u>Scowlicious</u>
The unhappy face your
Cheattymoggy makes when you
present them with anything less than
the smoked salmon and beluga
caviar they've had next door. Usually
accompanied by a Disgustiprowl.

<u>Sharplesoft</u>
That unnerving moment when a cat touches you gently with extended claws and gazes at you with a mix of affection and devilish amusement.

<u>Spitwash</u>
To clean your face by rubbing it with
a paw covered in a thin layer of spit.
(Hmm! Does this really make a cat
cleaner?)

Strokestop
The useful way a cat flicks up its tail
to prevent your hand falling off its
back.

<u>Suitcat</u>
To be *Suitcatted* is to find your
heavily moulting cat curled up in
your half-packed suitcase full of
recently-cleaned clothes.

Sweetface

A look of nonchalant innocence
affected by a cat standing beside a
broken item as if to say, 'What me?
No, I didn't do that. I wasn't even
here until just now'.

<u>Tailhint</u>
The twitching of your cat's tail, which
indicates that any attempt at
affection will be met with a vicious
attack.

## Tauntfear

The regret and slight fear you feel
from having over-teased your cat
with a toy to the point it may decide
to get violent with you and not the
toy.

Telettack

When a cat assaults something on your TV screen.

Ticklelober
A cheeky human who likes to tease
felines by lightly prodding their ear
hairs.

<u>Tummyumtiousness</u>
The contentment derived from
tickling a cat's tummy.

<u>Warmgamble</u>
The lovely warm spot on the chair
where a cat has just sat, but which is
now covered in fur.

## Yowlhaunt
The alarm felt at hearing your cat
suddenly yowling in the middle of the
night. What can they hear that you
can't? Leaves you awake with
paranoia as they drift back to sleep.

## Zoolochum

The feeling of pure friendship that
exists between you and your animal
friend, which is, unlike your human
relationships, delightfully
uncomplicated.

## Acknowledgements

Thank you to: our agents Gaia and Lucy for all their support; to Rowan for letting us write about cats and dogs; our families for your love; to Tigger, Sox, Fenella and Perky for the fluffy cuddles.